Emerald Gemstones

A Collection of Historical Articles on the Origins, Structure, Properties and Uses of Emeralds

By

Various Authors

British Library Cataloguing-in-Publication Data
A catalogue record for this book is available from
the British Library

Introduction to Gemmology

Gemmology is the science dealing with natural and artificial gems and gemstones. It is considered a geoscience and a branch of mineralogy. Although some practice gemmology as a sole profession, often jewellers become academically trained gemmologists, qualified to identify and evaluate gems. Rudimentary education in gemmology for jewellers and gemmologists began in the nineteenth century, but the first qualifications were instigated after the 'National Association of Goldsmiths of Great Britain' (NAG), set up a Gemmological Committee for this purpose in 1908. This committee matured into the 'Gemmological Association of Great Britain' (also known as Gem-A), now an educational charity and accredited awarding body, with its courses taught worldwide. The first US graduate of Gem-A's Diploma Course, in 1929, was Robert Shipley who later established both the 'Gemmological Institute of America' and the 'American Gem Society'. There are now several professional schools and associations of gemmologists and certification programs around the world.

The first gemmological laboratory serving the jewellery trade was established in London in 1925, prompted by the influx of the newly developed 'cultured pearl' and advances in the synthesis of rubies and sapphires. There are now numerous Gem Labs around the world requiring ever more advanced equipment and experience to identify the new challenges - such as treatments to gems, new synthetics and other new materials. Gemstones are basically categorized based on of their crystal structure, specific gravity, refractive index and other optical properties such as pleochroism. The physical property of 'hardness' is defined by the non-linear 'Mohs Scale' of mineral hardness. Gemmologists study these factors while valuing or appraising cut and polished gemstones. Gemmological microscopic study of the internal structure is used to determine whether a gem is synthetic or natural, by revealing natural fluid inclusions and partially melted exogenous crystals, in order to demonstrate evidence of heat treatment to enhance colour. The spectroscopic analysis of cut gemstones also allows a gemmologist to understand the atomic structure and identify its origin; a major factor in valuing a gemstone. For example, a ruby from Burma will have definite internal and optical activity variance as compared to a Thai ruby.

Gem identification is basically a process of elimination. Gemstones of similar colour undergo non-destructive optical testing until there is only one possible identity. Any single test is indicative, only. For example, the specific gravity of ruby is 4.00, glass is 3.15-4.20, and cubic zirconia is 5.6-5.9. So, one can easily tell the difference between cubic zirconia and the other two; however, there is overlap between ruby and glass. And, as with all naturally occurring materials, no two gems are identical. The geological environment in which they are created influences the overall process, so that although the basics can be identified, the presence of chemical 'impurities' and substitutions along with structural imperfections vary - thus creating 'individuals.' Having said this, the three main methods of testing gems are highly successful in proper identification. These are:

- Identification by refractive index - This test determines the gems identity by measuring the refraction of light in the gem. Every material has a critical angle, at which point light is reflected back internally. This can be measured and thus used to determine the gem's identity. Typically, this is measured using a refractometer, although it is possible to measure it using a microscope.

- Identification by specific gravity – This method, also known as 'relative density', varies depending upon the chemical composition and crystal structure type. Heavy liquids with a known specific gravity are used to test loose gemstones. Specific gravity is measured by comparing the weight of the gem in air with the weight of the gem suspended in water.

- Identification by spectroscopy – This technique uses a similar principle to how a prism works, to separate white light into its component colours. A gemmological spectroscope is utilised to analyse the selective absorption of light in the gem material. Essentially, when light passes from one medium to another, it bends. Blue light bends more than red light. Depending on the gem material, it will adjust how much this light bends. Colouring agents or chromophores show bands in the spectroscope and indicate which element is responsible for the gem's colour.

Contents

EMERALD.

The emerald or green beryl is one of the most highly prized of the gem stones. Its magnificent color has rightly been compared to the color of the fresh grass in spring, and in brilliancy this stone far exceeds all other green gems, excepting only the very rare green corundrum or green sapphire.

The emerald is said to be very soft when first withdrawn from the mine, but it hardens by exposure to the air.

A perfect emerald of fair size is a rarity, so that the saying " an emerald without a flaw " has passed into a proverb.

This stone is so light, compared to a diamond or sapphire, that a carat emerald will be very much larger than either of the above stones.

The emerald is composed of :

Silica 68.50
Alumina 15.75
Glucina 12.50
Peroxide of iron . . 1.
Lime 0.25
Oxide of chrome . . 0.30
And traces of magnesia, of lime, and of soda.

The vivid green color of the emerald is supposed to come from the oxide of chrome, as the other beryls do not contain chrome.

Emeralds are found in New Granada, near Bogota, Egypt, East India, Burmah, Ural in Europe; Salzburg, Austria; Mt. Remarkable, South Australia; and North America. Some of the finest come from the mines of Muza, near Bogota, and the best stones are called Peruvian emeralds. During the conquest of Peru by the Spaniards, many very fine emeralds were destroyed by the invaders, who tested them by grinding and pounding, and concluded that the emeralds were worthless, because they were not as hard as the diamonds or sapphires.

In 1587, Joseph D'Acosta returned to Spain with two cases of emeralds, each case weighing one hundred pounds.

Green tourmaline sometimes passes for the emerald, but it is somewhat softer and considerably heavier.

Olivines or chrysolites, if of a fine green color, sometimes resemble the emerald, but they are much heavier than the emerald and have a fatty lustre. Green spinels are heavier and harder than emeralds.

THE IDENTIFICATION OF EMERALD

EMERALD SHARES WITH RUBY AND SAPPHIRE THE rank of "precious stone" in the popular estimation, and, as with the corundum gems, its rarity and costliness have served to stimulate man's ingenuity in providing artificial substitutes. Just as the red of ruby and the blue of sapphire cannot properly be matched by any other natural mineral, so is the pure emerald green unequalled by any other transparent natural gem-stone.

The synthesis of emerald has been achieved in Germany and introduced more recently in the U.S.A., by a method not lending itself to mass production (see p. 72). All the **synthetic emeralds** so far examined by the author and other scientific workers could be distinguished from natural stones by their lower density, lower refraction and birefringence, internal markings, etc. (Chapter VI.)

The most effective emerald substitutes are undoubtedly **Doublets** and **Pastes** both of which can be produced in colours which the unaided eye can hardly distinguish from that of the genuine stone and moreover can be ingeniously provided with flaws and internal markings which superficially resemble those associated with emerald. However deceptive in appearance these imitations may be, they are very easily detected by any of several simple scientific tests. The handiest and most rapidly applied test is to place the suspected stone under a strong electric light and to view it through a Chelsea colour filter held close to the eye. Fine emeralds will then appear an almost ruby red and any well-coloured emerald except those from South Africa, which show little colour change, will show a reddish hue, whereas green pastes and most doublets will retain a green appearance. This test, though not so scientifically infallible as more orthodox identification with the refractometer, etc., has the advantage that it can be used in examination of large parcels of stones or numbers of small stones set in an eternity ring which it would take considerable time to test by other methods. It can also be used on cabochon emeralds or emerald beads, for which the refractometer is not applicable. The only natural green stones which show a reddish tint under the filter are fluorspar, zircon, and

4

demantoid garnet. Of these the first-named, though rarely cut, has on occasion been taken for emerald, but it is not likely that either demantoid or zircon would deceive an experienced jeweller.

Emerald is a green beryl in which the colour is due to traces of chromic oxide. It is a feature of this colouring agent, which also causes the red in ruby and spinel and the betwixt-and-between colour of alexandrite, that even when it produces a green colour it transmits a proportion of deep red light. This is the reason why the stone appears red under the Chelsea filter which (in addition to a band in the yellow-green) also transmits light of similar deep red colour.

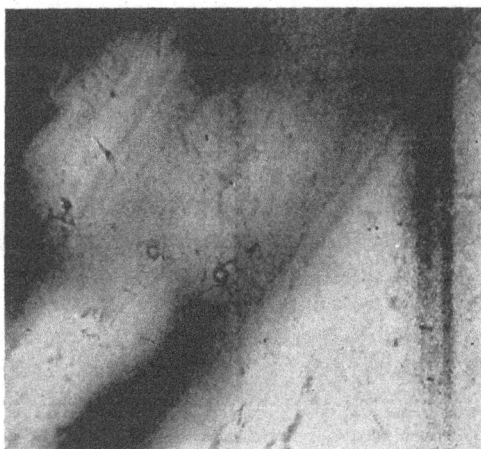

Fig. 39.—Three-phase Inclusions in Colombian Emerald.

Another consequence of the presence of chromium in emerald is the absorption spectrum which it displays, the presence of which proves the stone to be an emerald and also serves to differentiate true emerald beryl from beryls of the aquamarine series which owe their green colour to iron. The absorption spectrum of emerald has already been described and illustrated in Chapter VIII. The most striking features are a close pair of dark lines in the deep red with two fainter less clearly marked bands more towards the orange. There is some absorption of yellow, the extent of this broad absorption region depending upon the depth of colour of the stone and the crystallographic direction in which it is viewed. Having due regard to the appearance of the stone, the only variety which can possibly be confused with emerald when using the absorption spectrum test is fine translucent green jadeite, which also owes its colour to chromium and shows a rather similar series of bands, though not so clear-cut.

As for the other distinctive properties of emerald : the refractive indices for Colombian and Siberian stones average near 1·57 and 1·58, the birefringence being low—only ·006. The density for the finest emeralds is always near 2·71 ; thus they readily float in bromoform, unlike all other natural transparent green gem-stones. For South African emeralds the density and R.I. figures are somewhat higher than those just quoted, and for the pale emeralds from Brazil they are rather lower. The extreme range lies between 1·560 and 1·587 for the lower of the two refractive indices and 2·67 and 2·77 for the density.

Though such things may exist, the author has never yet encountered a *true* **Emerald Doublet**—that is, one consisting of two shallow pieces of emerald cemented together to form a more important whole. The cheap doublet with thin garnet top fused to a green glass base is sometimes seen, but the most successful imitation is the so-called **"Soudé Emerald"** made from a thin slice of emerald-green glass sandwiched between two thicker pieces of quartz, the quartz being specially chosen for its natural emerald-like feathers. In soudé emeralds the quartz-glass junctions usually occur at or near the girdle, and may thus be concealed in a set stone. The quartz provides a material with density, refractive index, and hardness only slightly below that of emerald, but on a refractometer there should be no doubt at all in the observer's mind, since quartz gives readings (1·544–1·553) quite distinctly lower than emerald, and in sodium light the birefringence is noticeably larger. Free from its setting, soudé emerald, in common with all other doublets, can of course be easily detected by viewing the composite stone sideways in a vessel of liquid, when the component parts can be clearly distinguished. If a density test be applied, the soudé doublet often shows surprisingly high values (an actual example being 2·88) considering that the bulk of the specimen consists of quartz (S.G. = 2·65). This indicates that a very heavy lead glass is used for the middle layer. In common with other doublets the soudé emerald shows under the microscope spherical bubbles at the junction layers.

6

Its green appearance under the Chelsea filter and lack of distinctive absorption bands are also discriminative features.

One interesting type of **Glass Imitation** which is occasionally used to simulate emerald is actually composed of fused beryl coloured with chromic oxide, thus having the chemical composition, though not the crystal structure, of emerald. Such specimens may form very good imitations so far as colour is concerned, and are harder than the normal run of glasses. The refractive index (near 1·52) and density (near 2·42) are, however, very much lower than for crystallized beryl, and included bubbles are always to be seen. The more ordinary **"Paste" Imitations** of emerald usually consist of rather soft lead glasses having refractive indices between 1·60 and 1·66 and densities between 3·40 and 4·00, though calcium glasses having much lower constants are sometimes used.

As already stated, no other transparent mineral displays the true emerald green. The rare enstatite and diopside from Kimberley and from Burma also owe their fine green partly to chromium, but their colour is none the less quite distinct from emerald. **Jadeite** ("Chinese" jade) does indeed sometimes achieve a true emerald green, but it is never properly transparent, and its peculiar shagreened surface is usually quite distinctive, apart from the fact that its constants are entirely different from those of beryl (see table).

Transparent green **Fluorspar** is occasionally cut, its colour closely approaches that of the pale emerald, and it appears reddish under the Chelsea colour filter. Nevertheless, it is easily distinguished from emerald by its low, single refraction, higher density, and inferior hardness. When in the form of beads or carvings the spectroscope provides a useful check. In place of the narrow chromium bands seen in the emerald spectrum, green fluorspar shows a rather vague band centred near 5850A in the yellow region. Fluorspar has a ready cleavage parallel to the octahedral planes. The cleavage surfaces are not very perfect and have a very typical appearance, by which the mineral may often be recognized. Even where no external cleavage breaks can be seen incipient cleavage flaws can usually be detected in fluorspar beads or ear-rings. Those who are fortunate enough to possess an ultra-violet lamp are probably familiar with the violet fluorescence which fluorspar of almost all colours so strikingly

7

displays. The very name fluorescence owes its origin to the mineral on account of this remarkable effect. Ultra-violet light therefore provides a rapid and beautiful means of confirming the identity of green fluorspar. Emerald tends to show a red fluorescence under the rays, the effect being particularly marked in the case of synthetic emerald.

Heat-treated green **Tourmalines** from Brazil provide pretty stones which the tyro may confuse with emerald, though any of the simple tests mentioned will serve to detect them. **Demantoid Garnets** often contain a trace of chromium and then have a fine colour—more yellowish green, however, than with emerald. The brilliant lustre and "fire" of demantoid in themselves are distinctive. **Green Sapphire** and **Green Zircon** need hardly be mentioned as serious rivals to emerald, though their properties are included in the comparative table for completeness' sake. The same may be said of **Peridot**, which has a distinctive yellowish-green colour of its own.

Finally, it should be mentioned that, though true synthetic emeralds are as yet only on the market in small quantities and small sizes, **Synthetic Corundum** and **Synthetic Spinel** are both manufactured in various shades of green. True emerald green, however, has not been achieved in these materials.

TABLE FOR IDENTIFYING GREEN STONES

Species.	H.	S.G.	R.I.	D.R.
Emerald	$7\frac{1}{2}$	2·71	1·57—1·58	·006
Zircon	7	4·0*	1·82*	·01*
Sapphire	9	4·00	1·76—1·77	·009
Demantoid	$6\frac{1}{2}$	3·85	1·89	none
Peridot	$6\frac{1}{2}$	3·34	1·65—1·69	·037
Jadeite	7	3·33	1·65—1·67	·014
Fluorspar.	4	3·18	1·43	none

*The constants for Green Zircon are very variable.

The lovely deep green emerald is the queen gem of the mineral family known as *beryl,* just as the ruby and sapphire are the royal members of the *corundum* family. Oddly enough, the chromium oxide which is the coloring agent of rubies is the same one which imparts the green to emeralds. As the semiprecious "fancy sapphires" are related to the ruby and sapphire so the aquamarine and golden beryl are the lesser relatives of the emerald, the hierarchy dependent on color. A beryl stone may be the most beautiful *pale* green in the world but it is not an emerald—it is an aquamarine.

Like the corundum gems, emeralds crystallize in the hexagonal system but they are somewhat softer, having a hardness of 7½-8 on Mohs' scale. An "emerald without a flaw" is extremely rare. In fact these gems are characterized by an elaborate network of thin, vein-like cracks which usually cross one another in more or less haphazard fashion. The gem cutter must be extraordinarily skillful to eliminate these and the cloudy, discolored portions which are almost always found. When a truly flawless, large emerald is found it becomes a museum treasure or a wealthy collector's item and seldom reaches the jeweler's counter where it could command a price as high as $10,000 a carat. Some of the finest and largest, of course, found their way into the crown jewels of various governments. Russia particularly gloried in her crown emeralds before the present regime took over the reins. Many of these were obtained from mines in the Ural Mountains near Ekaterinburg. Whether these mines are still worked is not known at the present time.

But the world's finest emeralds now come from the mines around Muzo, Colombia. These are particularly identifiable because they contain cubic crystals of rock salt quite unlike anything seen in other genuine emeralds. The first of these South American mines was dis-

Cabochon cut emeralds as pendants on a French heirloom court diamond necklace re-executed by Van Cleef & Arpels.

9

covered by accident in 1558, and proved to be one of the so-called lost mines of the Incas, that reticent tribe whose members refused to disclose to the conquering Spaniards the source of their magnificent "green riches." The Muzo emerald mines are operated by the Colombian Government.

An even older source of emeralds is Egypt where the mines once belonging to Queen Cleopatra still provide gems of fair quality. Cleopatra, of course, enhanced her beauty with the green gems and was noted for giving them to ambassadors. Frequently she had her portrait engraved upon them and many of the emeralds worn in Roman times are believed to have come from Cleopatra's mines.

Emeralds may be perfectly transparent or entirely opaque. The latter were once favored for cameos. One choice specimen of the emerald cameo was obtained in 1928 by Arthur Silberfeld of New York, an importer of precious stones. This is a carving of the head of Julius Caesar on a solid piece of emerald weighing 225 carats, once a prized possession of the Bonaparte family. Before the sculptor, Henri August Burdy, started to work on it, the piece weighed more than 1,000 carats in the rough.

One of the world's greatest treasures is the gold and emerald crown of Our Lady of the Andes once owned by the Roman Catholic Cathedral of Popayan, Colombia. This is a massive crown made of pure gold and containing what is said to be the largest collection of fine emeralds in the world—453 jewels with a combined weight of 1,500 carats. Spanish goldsmiths were commissioned to make it in 1593 as a votive offering from the city to the Virgin Mary and they were instructed that "the crown must exceed in beauty, in grandeur and in value the crown of any reigning monarch on earth, else it would not be a becoming gift for the Queen of Heaven." Six years later, in 1599, the crown was completed.

Emerald lovers have included Queen Isabella, Empress Josephine, Empress Eugenie, the Maharajah of Kashmir, the Maharajah of Patiala, and the Duchess of Windsor. One of the best American collections is that of Mrs. Harrison Williams, for years popularly regarded as the best dressed woman in the world.

The cool grass green depths of an emerald make it the most restful gem in existence. Perhaps the greatest tribute ever paid it was when the Irish, with their appreciation of beauty and rarity, elected to call their beloved land the "Emerald Isle."

EMERALD

(Hardness, 7¾; specific gravity, 2·69 to 2·80;
refractive indices, 1·57–1·58)

THIS stone, the most costly of all gem stones at present
on the market, is the beautiful velvety green variety
of beryl, a silicate of aluminium and beryllium. Aquamarine, golden beryl, and morganite (the pink variety)
are all beryls also, and are chemically of the same
composition as emerald, though they differ in colour.
The green in emerald is probably due to a small percentage of chromic oxide, as heat does not affect the
colour.

Crystals frequently occur in the form of hexagonal
prisms (hexagonal system), and are nearly always
found flawed. This, in contrast to aquamarine, which
is usually found in comparatively large and flawless
pieces, is one reason why fine emeralds are so expensive.
Most emeralds are marred by cracks and inclusions,
which greatly lessen their value. Pale shades are not
so valuable, and the best colours range from a deep
velvet green to a grass green. The vitreous lustre
of a good stone gives a beautiful velvety appearance.

Emerald shows little cleavage, and its degree of
hardness is rather low for such an expensive stone.
It has a low specific gravity, so it is comparatively
light in weight. Stones are very brittle, and great care
must be taken when setting into jewellery. For this
reason the girdle should never be cut too thinly.
Dichroism is distinct in well-coloured specimens.
Emerald is usually step cut, and ring and brooch
stones are nearly always seen in this form. Acids have
no effect on this stone, though it may be fused by
means of a blow pipe.

Emeralds are rarely, if ever, found in gravels, but
usually in the parent rock, which is often a mica schist.

11

The chief localities are Colombia (South America), Egypt, the Urals, and New South Wales. It is interesting to note that some crystals from the Colombian mines appear to be clear and transparent when taken from the mine, but flaw immediately on exposure to the air. Some stones even splinter into fragments.

The word "emerald" is derived from a Sanskrit word, though originally it was applied to a different green stone (chrysocolla). It was not discovered that emerald was a beryl until about a century ago. The emeralds known to the Ancients all came from the mines in Upper Egypt, situated in the range of mountains running parallel to the western side of the Red Sea. These mines are still worked, although they produce rather poor stones. The ruins of these mines were re-discovered by the French explorer Caillaud about one hundred years ago. He found tools and plant there which showed that the mines dated many centuries back. Many of the ancient emerald scarabs came from here, as also did the famous engraved stone which was presented to Cleopatra. This area was also the source of supply of all emeralds mentioned in the Bible.

The Uralian mines were accidentally discovered by a Russian peasant in the year 1830. Though some large stones have been found, they are not so fine as those from Colombia, where they have been mined for many centuries. The fine emeralds which Cortez presented to his wife were of extraordinary size and quality. These stones, which were carved and inscribed, were unfortunately lost at sea in the year 1529. Some of the best stones were no doubt carried off by the Spaniards amongst other spoils from South America. However, it was some time before they discovered the actual mines, as the natives persistently refused to disclose the secret of their situation. In 1558 they were discovered by accident, and they were subsequently actively worked.

From time to time the working of the mines has been continued in a spasmodic way owing to difficulties with the local government, with labour, and with clima conditions. Lately the mining rights were leased to a syndicate by the Colombian Government. Disagreement about details led to litigation between the government and the syndicate, and for some time working was suspended. Meanwhile, demand for good stones increased, and prices rose considerably. The rough stones mined during the law proceedings accumulated and were lodged for safety with a bank in London. On the settlement of the case, the rough was offered for sale, but owing to the enormous sum involved, it was possible for only a limited number of firms to consider the purchase. The stones were eventually bought by a French firm, who had them cut and then mounted in the most suitable forms of jewellery. By ingenious methods, demand for emeralds was further stimulated, and now enormous prices are being obtained for good stones. The contract under which the French firm marketed the stones was terminated in 1928, and now the Government have assumed sole control, selling direct to dealers. Very little has been produced since 1930.

The actual mining in South America has always been performed by Indians. The area is a region of about 4,000 square miles, but the only mine being worked at present is the Muzo, 92 miles north-west of Bogota. Other centres are Coscuez and Somondoco (or Chivor), but all those places are situated at high altitudes and in most inaccessible and rugged districts. The surrounding dense tropical jungle renders the mining of the precious mineral very difficult; transport, except by mule, is almost impossible.

The workers live at these centres in buildings which are provided for them, and they are closely watched by police to prevent thieving. Working is by the open system, although formerly tunnelling was the form of operation. The loose soil is separated from the emeralds by a dry method and not by the use of water. The vegetation has first to be cleared, and then the soil, to a depth of about three feet, is worked in terrace form. The emerald-bearing calcite veins are removed by hand, sorted and washed. The precious stones are then picked out and graded; those from Muzo are sent to Bogota under Government seal by mule. A normal output for one year would be about 800,000 carats, but most of this would be of small size and of poor quality.

In December, 1929, a company was formed to exploit emerald mines discovered in 1927 in the Leysdorp district in South Africa. The stones, with other varieties of beryl, occur in mica-schist, and are accompanied by tourmaline, quartz, apatite, felspar, and molybdenite. They are usually cracked, flawed, and of a cloudy colour, but a few fine stones producing £100 per carat have been cut from material found here. Most of the stones, however, are only suitable for cutting en cabochon or in the form of beads. Other new stones which come on to the market emanate from Russia and South-West Africa. The Russian stones are nearly always pale in colour, whilst the African material is a dark, bluish green with many flaws.

An emerald mine near Salzburg (Austria) dates back to Roman times, and in the past it produced many good stones. In the year 1896 it was acquired by a British company, who sold it in 1913 to a group of local workers. The mine was advertised for sale in 1928, so evidently no great wealth of stones is to be found there now.

Another unimportant source of supply, since 1913, is Brazil, but only pale and flawed stones in small quantities have been found. Also from 1927 to 1929 a few stones were mined in the Poona district in West Australia, but these were of no commercial note.

Actual rarity is the chief cause of the value of emeralds, though no doubt fine stones are really beautiful, and of all the green stones that exist none can approach the beauty of the velvety-green emerald. Also, unlike most green stones, emeralds retain their colour in artificial light. Even in the days of Pliny this stone was highly esteemed, for he wrote of emeralds, "Neither dim nor shade, nor yet the light of a candle, causes them to lose their lustre."

The largest single crystal of emerald known belongs to the Duke of Devonshire. It is nearly a regular hexagon, and is about two inches in diameter and length. It weighs about one thousand three hundred and forty-seven carats, but though of good colour it is badly flawed. The stone was given to the Duke by Dom Pedro of Brazil.

The finest cut stone belonged to the late Czar of Russia. This weighed about thirty carats.

A fine crystal and also a cut stone may be seen in the British Museum (Mineral Gallery).

EMERALD

47.—What is an emerald?

A precious stone of high rank in the world of gems and also in the scale of worth; beloved of the engraver, a joy to the lover of colour, and an inspiration to the lover of words. Look into the depths of an emerald and you can visualise rich green lawns in spring and cool valleys in summer. There is only one colour for an emerald, a soft, velvety green, and only one green known as emerald. It is a stone which belongs to the beryl group of gems and is closely related to the aquamarine.

48.—Why are emeralds so costly ? Are they so rare ?

Emeralds are by no means rare, they are in fact found in great quantities, but such a large percentage are faulty to the extent of being useless for jewellery that when good stones come to light they are expensive, and when perfectly clear and quite flawless emeralds are found their rarity makes them more costly than diamonds (again weight for weight).

49.—Is the engraving of emeralds an old or a new idea ?

Records prove that from ancient times the emerald has been a medium of the engraver's art and skill. Cleopatra was presented with a fine engraved emerald. Pliny tells of one given to Lucullus by Ptolemy, King of Egypt, with his portrait engraved on it. The Egyptians carved emeralds into scarabs, and the Indians shaped them into Hindu gods.

50.—Where are emeralds found ?

They come from many places: Russia, Australia, Brazil, South Africa, South America, Siberia, but the most famous of all are from the Muzo mines in Colombia.

51.—How are emeralds cut or fashioned ?

When not engraved they are usually trap or table cut. When fashioned as brilliants it is to hide flaws.

52.—Has the emerald any special virtue or meaning ?

It is a gem which should be especially dear to the hearts of women, for it stands for success and happiness in marriage. Hence the couplet:

" No happier wife and mother in the land
Than she with emerald shining on her hand."

EMERALD

The grass green variety of the mineral beryl, which since the days of Pliny has been called emerald (see color plate frontispiece), is today the supreme high point in gem values, having by reason of popular mode, which demands green rather than red stones, outranked even the ruby in this respect. The source of this color is said to be very small percentages of chromic oxides present in the silicate of aluminium and beryllium, which compose all the stones belonging to the beryl mineralogical family. Crystals of beryl occur in six-sided prisms whose ends are terminated either by single planes at right angles to the prism edges or by flat six-sided pyramids or by a combination of both of these modifications. In hardness the beryl gems, which include the emerald, are somewhat softer than rubies and sapphires, approaching dangerously near the limit at which a facetted gem stone may be used in ring mounts without showing undue wear on the edges.

Queen Cleopatra had an emerald mine that is still in existence near the shore of the Red Sea in Upper Egypt, although no emeralds are found there at present. It was perhaps from this place that the celebrated emerald through which Nero viewed the gladiatorial games came, and no doubt many of the gems of the ancient world are traceable to this source.

Emeralds have long been the glory of the Russian crown jewels. Their deep rich greens appealed to the almost barbaric love of splendor that underlies Russian taste, and they were, moreover, to be found in Russian territory, on the Asiatic side of the Ural Mountains near Ekaterinburg.

Both Egyptian and Russian emeralds occur in micaceous schists and gneisses, the gem crystals in general exhibiting flaws and "feathers" which materially detract from the value of the cut stones. A similar schist-like rock at Habachtal, in the Salzburg Alps, has produced a small amount of inferior emeralds. Also the micaceous gneiss of North Carolina has furnished material from which a few small stones have been cut. The great source of emeralds of our own day is the now famous mine in the vicinity of Muso in the republic of Colombia. The story of South American emeralds is a romantic one. When the Spaniards conquered Peru and took from the Incas all their treasured wealth, they found an immense number of emeralds, some of almost incredible size, in the temples and on the persons of the conquered natives. Thus was Europe soon flooded with what were then called Spanish or Peruvian emeralds, although none of them came originally either from Spain or Peru. But neither persecution nor torture could induce the unfortunate Incas to reveal the source of their wealth of green stones, and it was only by accident that in 1558 one of the native emerald mines was found near Muso in Colombia. The natives had destroyed all traces of the others, and the thick, impenetrable, tropical jungle had swallowed them up. The Muso mine has been producing emeralds periodically ever since, and in quality of color and freedom from imperfections they are far superior to stones from other sources. About three decades ago another of the lost emerald mines of the Incas was rediscovered at Sonondoco, not far from Muso. The stones from this locality are said to be of not so fine a quality as those from the latter mine. At Muso, as well as at Sonondoco, the emeralds occur in a crystalline limestone.

HEXAGONAL SYSTEM

HOLOHEDRAL DIVISION

Symmetry.

The holohedral division of the hexagonal system is characterized by the presence of one principal and six secondary symmetry planes which lie at right angles to the principal symmetry plane. The secondary symmetry planes are arranged in two groups each of which contains three planes. The planes of each group intersect each other at angles of 90° and 120°, and are interchangeable; while the planes of one group are non-interchangeable with those of the other group which they intersect at angles of 30°, 90°, or 150°.

Selection, Position, and Designation of the Crystal Axes.

The principal symmetry axis is chosen as one of the crystal axes, is held vertically, and is called the *c* axis. *Three* other crystal axes are so selected as to coincide with either group of interchangeable secondary symmetry axes. One is held horizontally from right to left. The other two will, then, be horizontal, but will make angles of 60° with each other as well as with the right and left axis (see Fig. 24). Since all three horizontal axes are interchangeable, they are all called *a* axes. None of the horizontal axes is interchangeable with the vertical axis.

This is the only system in which more than three crystal axes are used. While it would be possible to determine the holohedral forms by the use of three

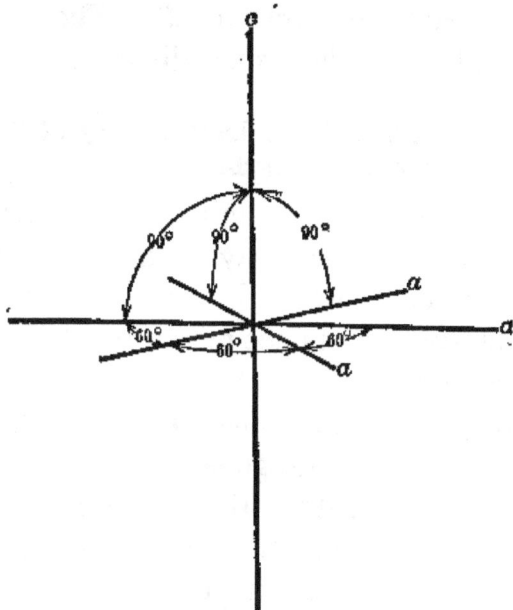

Fig. 24. — Crystal axes of the hexagonal system.

non-interchangeable axes intersecting at right angles, as in the orthorhombic system (see p. 103), this would make it necessary to attach different names to faces identically of the same shape and size, and would in no way suggest the six- or three-fold arrangement of faces which distinguishes this system. It would further necessitate the devising of new rules for developing hemihedral and tetartohedral forms; and would lead to so many difficulties that it is far simpler to use the three interchangeable horizontal axes than two non-interchangeable ones.

23

Orienting Crystals.

Holohedral hexagonal forms are oriented by holding the principal symmetry plane horizontally, and either set of interchangeable secondary symmetry planes in such a way that one of the planes will extend vertically from right to left. The crystal axes will then extend in the proper directions.

The Law of Rationality or Irrationality of Ratios Between Unit Axial Lengths.

The ratio between two unit axial lengths on non-interchangeable axes is always an irrational quantity; while the ratio between the unit axial lengths on interchangeable axes is not only a rational quantity, but equals unity.

The law just stated, which applies to all systems, indicates that in the hexagonal system $a : c$ is always an irrational quantity. If a be taken as unity, which is always done, c may be greater or less than unity, but is always an irrational quantity, and is usually given to four decimal places. As an illustration, consider the hexagonal mineral beryl, of which emerald is a variety. The ground-form of this mineral cuts two of the horizontal and the vertical axes at such distances from the origin as will make the ratio between a and c as 1 is to 0.4989 (nearly). The unit axial distances of this mineral are, then, $a = 1$ and $c = 0.4989$ (nearly). The value of c differs more or less for all hexagonal minerals. It is, then, a distinguishing characteristic of each hexagonal mineral.

Since m and n are always rational quantities (see p. 15), it follows that $na : c$ and $a : mc$ are irrational quantities; while $a : na$ is a rational quantity.

In all systems but the isometric m may be less than unity; and it is customary to apply this parameter (m) to the unit axial length of the *vertical* axis. n must be greater than unity in the hexagonal and isometric systems only.

First Order Position Defined.

Forms with faces whose planes cut two horizontal axes equally (at equal finite distances from the origin), and are parallel to the third horizontal axis, are said to be in the first order position.

Second Order Position Defined.

Forms with faces whose planes cut two of the horizontal axes equally and the third horizontal axis at a distance from the origin which is half that cut off on the other two horizontal axes are said to be in the second order position.

Third Order Position Defined.

Forms with faces whose planes cut all three horizontal axes unequally are said to be in the third order position.

Holohedral Hexagonal Forms Tabulated.

Name.	Symbol.	Number of faces.
1st order pyramid (Fig. 25)	$a:a:\infty a:mc$	12
1st order prism (Fig. 26)	$a:a:\infty a:\infty c$	6
2nd order pyramid (Fig. 27)	$2a:a:2a:mc$	12
2nd order prism (Fig. 28)	$2a:a:2a:\infty c$	6
Dihexagonal pyramid (Fig. 29)	$na:a:pa:mc$	24
Dihexagonal prism (Fig. 30)	$na:a:pa:\infty c$	12
Basal-pinacoid (Fig. 31)	$\infty a:\infty a:\infty a:c$	2.

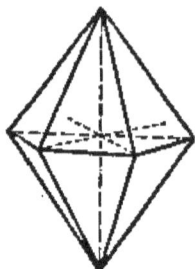

FIG. 25.—1st order pyramid.   FIG. 26. — 1st order prism.

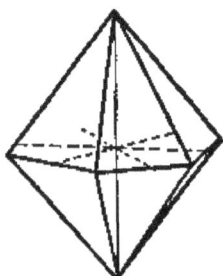

FIG. 27.—2nd order pyramid.   FIG. 28. — 2nd order prism.

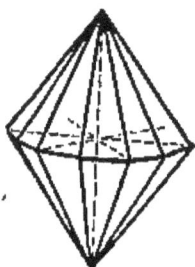

FIG. 29.— Dibexagonal   FIG. 30. — Dibexagonal
pyramid.   prism.

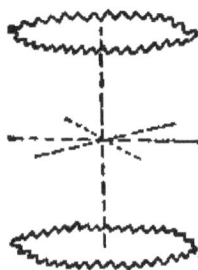

FIG. 31. — Basal pinacoid.

Synonyms for the Names of the Holohedral Hexagonal Forms.

1st order pyramid — 1st order bipyramid, or unit pyramid.

1st order prism — unit prism.

2nd order pyramid — 2nd order bipyramid.

2nd order prism — none.

Dihexagonal pyramid — dihexagonal bipyramid.

Dihexagonal prism — none.

Basal-pinacoid — basal plane.

Method of Determining Holohedral Hexagonal Forms by the Use of Symbols.

After properly orienting the crystal in the manner already described select any face and ascertain the relative distances at which its plane intersects the four crystal axes, [remembering that no face or faces extended can cut the vertical axis at the same distance from the origin as it cuts any of the horizontal axes.] If, for instance, it appears that the plane of the face selected intersects all four of the axes, but that the three horizontal axes are all cut at unequal distances from the origin, the symbol of that face (and of the form of which it is a part) is $na : a : pa : mc$. By referring to the table of holohedral hexagonal forms (which should be memorized as soon as possible) it is seen that the form is the dihexagonal pyramid. If more than one form is represented on the crystal, each may be determined in the same way.

The parameter p in the symbol of the dihexagonal pyramid and prism is not an independent variable, but is, in fact, equal to $\dfrac{n}{n-1}$. When n equals 3, for instance, p will equal $\frac{3}{2}$ or $1\frac{1}{2}$. It might be better always to use $\frac{n}{n-1}$ instead of p, but, if the equality of the two symbols is always borne in mind, no confusion need result.

It is necessary to write the symbol of hexagonal forms in such a way as will make the second part of each symbol always a (or ∞a in the case of the basal-pinacoid). Thus, $na : a : pa : mc$ is correct, while $na : pa : a : mc$ is incorrect; and $a : 2a : 2a : mc$ is not the symbol of the 2nd order pyramid, while $2a : a : 2a : mc$ is the correct symbol of this form.

Suggestions for Attaining Facility in the Recognition of Forms.

Orient the crystal and determine which of the following descriptions (which should be learned at once) apply to the faces of different shape or size seen.

1st order pyramid: A face sloping down from the vertical axis directly towards the observer.

1st order prism: A vertical face extending from right to left.

2nd order pyramid: A face sloping down from the vertical axis directly to the right or left.

A 2nd order pyramid differs in no way from a 1st order pyramid excepting in position with respect to the horizontal crystal axes; and a twelve-faced pyramid may be placed in either the 1st or 2nd order position at will. Such a pyramid may, then, be considered either a 1st or a 2nd order pyramid depending upon the set of interchangeable symmetry axes with which the crystal axes are chosen to coincide. It is only when forms in both the 1st and 2nd order position occur on the same crystal that it is necessary to distinguish between 1st and 2nd order pyramids.

2nd order prism: A vertical face extending from front to back.

As is the case with the 2nd order pyramid, a 2nd order prism differs in no way from a 1st order prism

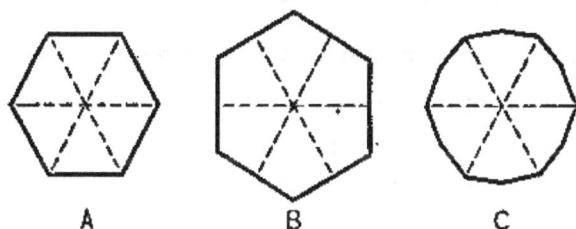

A   B   C

Fig. 32. — Diagrams showing relations of the 1st order (A), 2nd order (B), and dihexagonal (C) pyramids and prisms to the horizontal crystal axes.

excepting in position with respect to the horizontal crystal axes; and all that was said in the preceding section relative to the 2nd order pyramid applies with equal truth to the 2nd order prism.

It is customary to select the horizontal crystal axis in such a way as will place the largest and most prominent twelve-faced pyramid or six-faced prism in the 1st order position.

Pyramids and prisms intersecting in horizontal edges are always of the same order.

Dihexagonal pyramid: A face sloping down from the vertical axis in such a way that its plane intersects all three horizontal crystal axes at unequal finite distances from the origin.

29

Dihexagonal prism: A vertical face whose plane intersects all three horizontal crystal axes at unequal finite distances from the origin.

Basal-pinacoid: A horizontal face on top of a crystal.

Fixed and Variable Forms.

The only fixed holohedral hexagonal forms are the 1st and 2nd order prisms and the basal-pinacoid, and forms derived therefrom.

Fixed Angles of the Hexagonal System.

The only fixed angles in this system are those between the fixed forms just mentioned, namely, 90°, 120° (or 60°), and 150° (or 30°).

Miscellaneous.

The general statements made in the discussion of the holohedral division of the isometric system

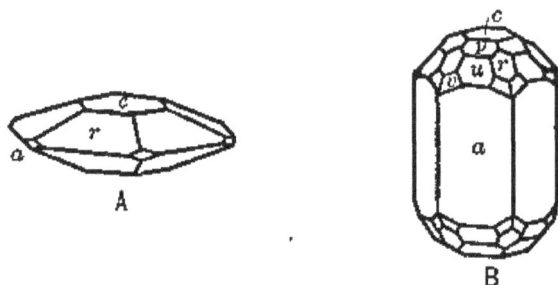

FIG. 33. — Holohedral hexagonal crystals.

A: Basal-pinacoid (*c*), 1st order pyramid (*r*), and 2nd order prism (*a*).

B: Basal-pinacoid (*c*), 1st order prism (*a*), two 1st order pyramids (*p* and *u*), 2nd order pyramid (*r*), and dihexagonal pyramid (*v*).

regarding combination of forms, determination of the number of forms, repetition of forms on a crystal, and limiting forms applies with equal truth to all the divisions of the hexagonal system. It may be mentioned, however, that repetitions of the same variable form are very common in the hexagonal system, and crystal models showing such repeated forms are not difficult to obtain.

RHOMBOHEDRAL HEMIHEDRAL DIVISION

Development or Derivation of the Forms.

Rhombohedral hemihedral hexagonal forms may be conceived to be developed by dividing each of the holohedral forms by means of the principal symmetry plane and *the set of interchangeable secondary symmetry planes containing the crystal axes* into twelve parts, or dodecants, then suppressing all faces lying wholly within alternate parts thus obtained, and extending the remaining faces until they meet in edges or corners.

Symmetry.

Rhombohedral hemihedral forms possess three interchangeable secondary symmetry planes which intersect along a common line at angles of 60° or 120°.

Selection, Position, and Designation of the Crystal Axes.

The three directions used as crystal axes in the holohedral division are still utilized for the same purpose in the rhombohedral hemihedral division. In other words, the vertical or c axis lies at the intersection of the three secondary symmetry planes; while the three interchangeable crystallographic directions used as horizontal or a axes are so held that one of them extends from right to left, and each of them bisects an angle between two of the secondary symmetry planes.

Orienting Crystals.

Rhombohedral hemihedral forms are oriented by holding a symmetry plane vertically *from front to back*, then rotating the crystal around the axis perpendicular to this plane until two other symmetry planes making angles of 60° to 120° with the plane first mentioned are held vertically. The crystal axes will then extend in the proper directions.

Rhombohedral Hemihedral Hexagonal Forms Tabulated.

Name.	Symbol.	Number of faces.	Form from which derived.
± Rhombohedron (Fig. 34)	$\pm \dfrac{a : a : \infty a : mc}{2}$	6	1st order pyramid
Hexagonal scalenohedron (Fig. 35)	$\dfrac{na : a : pa : mc}{2}$	12	dihexagonal pyramid
1st order prism (Fig. 26)....	$\dfrac{a : a : \infty a : \infty c}{2}$	6	1st order prism
2nd order pyramid (Fig. 27).	$\dfrac{2a : a : 2a : mc}{2}$	12	2nd order pyramid
2nd order prism (Fig. 28)...	$\dfrac{2a : a : 2a : \infty c}{2}$	6	2nd order prism
Dihexagonal prism (Fig. 30)	$\dfrac{na : a : pa : \infty c}{2}$	12	dihexagonal prism
Basal-pinacoid (Fig. 31)....	$\dfrac{\infty a : \infty a : \infty a : c}{2}$	2	basal-pinacoid

Synonyms for the Names of the Rhombohedral Hemihedral Hexagonal Forms.

Rhombohedron — none.

Scalenohedron — none.

Positive and Negative Forms Distinguished.

All those forms produced by the suppression of faces lying within the *same set* of alternating dodecants are said to be of the same sign (+ or −). It is customary to consider those forms with faces

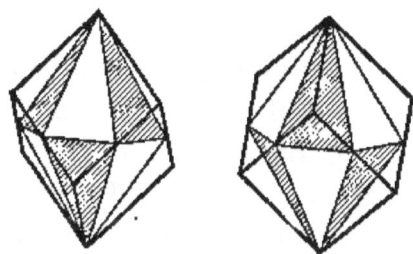

FIG. 34. — Positive (on left) and negative (on right) rhombohedrons containing the forms from which they are derived. The suppressed faces are shaded.

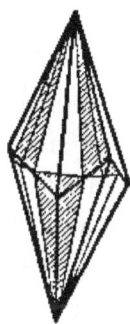

FIG. 35. — Hexagonal scalenohedron containing the form from which it is derived. The suppressed faces are shaded.

largely or entirely included within the upper dodecant directly facing the observer as +, while those with faces in the upper dodecant. at the back of the crystal furthest from the observer are −. In reality a + rhombohedron differs in no way from a − rhombohedron excepting in position; and a rhombohedron may be held in either the + or − position at will. It is customary to hold a crystal in such a way as to bring the largest and most prominent rhombohedron face principally or entirely into the upper dodecant facing the observer, which will make this form a + one. It is possible, but unnecessary, to distinguish between + and − hexagonal scalenohedrons.

If the sign of a form is not specifically stated as being $-$, it is always assumed that the form is $+$.

The forms on a crystal may all be of the same sign, or $+$ and $-$ forms may be combined.

Method of Determining Rhombohedral Hemihedral Hexagonal Forms by the Use of Symbols.

After properly orienting the crystal all the forms but the rhombohedron and scalenohedron may be easily identified by applying the rules already given for the determination of holohedral forms of the same name. The two hemihedral forms new in shape may be recognized by determining the symbol of any face in the manner described in the discussion of holohedral forms, dividing the symbol by 2, and then ascertaining from the table the name of the form possessing this symbol.

Suggestions for Attaining Facility in the Recognition of Forms.

Orient the crystal and determine which of the following descriptions (which should be learned at once) apply to the face or faces of different shape or size seen. It is assumed that the student is already familiar with the rules for recognizing those forms identical in shape with the holohedral ones (see p. 51).

$+$ *Rhombohedron:* A face sloping down from the vertical axis directly toward the observer. A rhombohedron has three faces at each end of the vertical axis so arranged that a face on top is directly above an edge below.

$-$ *Rhombohedron:* A face sloping down from the vertical axis directly away from the observer, at the back of the crystal.

Hexagonal scalenohedron: A face sloping down from the vertical axis in such a way that its plane intersects all three horizontal crystal axes at unequal finite distances from the origin.

The hexagonal scalenohedron is most readily confused with the 2nd order pyramid. To distinguish them, it should be remembered that the upper and lower faces of the latter always intersect in horizontal edges, and that the interfacial angles of the 2nd order pyramid, measured across edges converging towards the vertical axis, are all equal. Neither statement is true as regards the hexagonal scalenohedron.

Rules and Conventions Relating to Rhombohedrons.

As may be gathered from the statements already made in this volume (see p. 13), the unit rhombohedron in the case of any given mineral species is usually the rhombohedron occurring most commonly on crystals of that mineral. In the case of rhombohedral minerals with a well-developed rhombohedral cleavage (see p. 142), however, it is sometimes found more convenient to select the cleavage rhombohedron as the unit rhombohedron, and to call all distances at which this unit rhombohedron cuts the a and c axes the unit axial distances a and c. a is made equal to unity, and c is then some irrational quantity either greater or less than unity. It is customary to designate the unit rhombohedron by the symbol R which may be $+$ or $-$ according to its position on the crystal.

All other rhombohedrons than R will cut the a and c axes at such distances that if a is made equal to unity, mc will be some rational multiple of c. If m is equal to 2, the rhombohedron is represented by the symbol 2 R, either $+$ or $-$; while if m is equal to $\frac{1}{2}$, the rhombohedron is represented by the symbol $\frac{1}{2}$ R, either $+$ or $-$. Similarly, a rhombohedron intersecting the vertical axis at $3c$ may be represented by the symbol 3 R, etc.

It may be readily proved geometrically (although to offer such a proof is beyond the scope of this work) that any rhombohedron which truncates the edges of another rhombohedron will intersect

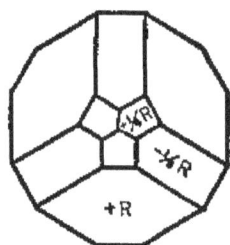

FIG. 36. — View from above of a unit rhombohedron, with its edges truncated by $-\frac{1}{2}R$, and the edges of the latter truncated by $+\frac{1}{4}R$.

the vertical axis at one-half the c value of the truncated rhombohedron and will be of opposite sign. In other words, $+$ R may have its edges truncated by $-\frac{1}{2}$ R; $-\frac{1}{2}$ R may have its edges truncated by $+\frac{1}{4}$ R, etc. Stated differently, $-\frac{1}{2}$ R will truncate the edges of $+$ R; or -2 R will truncate the edges of $+4$ R.

From what has been said it is evident that a $+$ rhombohedron always truncates a $-$ rhombohedron or vice versa. In order to ascertain whether one rhombohedron is truncating another, it is only necessary to determine whether one rhombohedron intersects the other in parallel edges. If a rhombohedron is intersected by other rhombohedron faces of opposite sign so as to produce parallel edges, the former is truncating the latter. Fig. 36 illustrates a crystal viewed from above that shows $+$ R, $-\frac{1}{2}$ R, and $+\frac{1}{4}$ R. If the rhombohedron represented in the case just mentioned as $-\frac{1}{2}$ R be taken as the unit rhombohedron, $+$ R, the other rhombohedrons shown will be -2 R and $-\frac{1}{2}$ R, respectively.

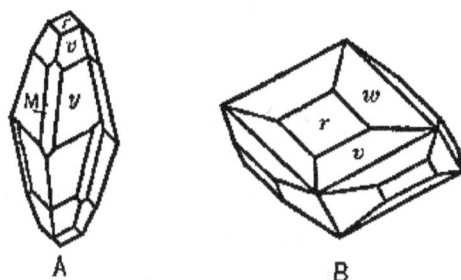

FIG. 37. — Rhombohedral hemihedral hexagonal crystals.

A: Two $+$ rhombohedrons (r and M) and two scaleno-hedrons (y and v).

B: $+$ rhombohedron (r) and two scalenohedrons (w and v).

PYRAMIDAL HEMIHEDRAL DIVISION

Development or Derivation of the Forms.

Pyramidal hemihedral hexagonal forms may be conceived to be developed by dividing each of the holohedral forms by means of all six secondary symmetry planes into twelve parts, then suppressing all faces lying wholly within alternate parts thus obtained, and extending the remaining faces until they meet in edges or corners.

Symmetry.

Pyramidal hemihedral forms possess only one symmetry plane which is in the position of the principal symmetry plane existing in the holohedral division. It is, however, in the pyramidal hemi-hedral division a secondary rather than a principal symmetry plane since there are no interchangeable symmetry planes perpendicular to it.

Pyramidal hemihedral hexagonal forms are, then, characterized by the presence of one secondary symmetry plane, and a general six-fold arrangement of faces.

Selection, Position, and Designation of the Crystal Axes.

The vertical or c crystal axis is made to coincide with the secondary symmetry axis. Three interchangeable horizontal axes parallel to prominent crystallographic directions at angles of 60° or 120° to each other are also selected, and one of these is so placed as to extend from right to left. Being interchangeable, all are called a axes.

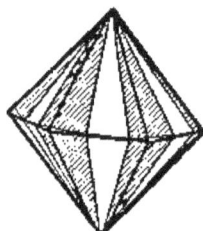

FIG. 38. — 3rd order pyramid containing the form from which it is derived. Suppressed faces are shaded.

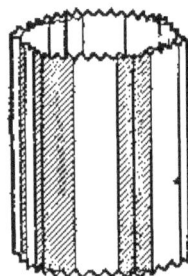

FIG. 39. — 3rd order prism containing the form from which it is derived. Suppressed faces are shaded.

Orienting Crystals.

The secondary symmetry plane is held horizontally. The crystal is then rotated around the symmetry axis until the most prominent pyramid or prism lies in the first order position. The crystal axes will then extend in the proper directions.

Pyramidal Hemihedral Hexagonal Forms Tabulated.

Name.	Symbol.	Number of faces.	Form from which derived.
3rd order pyramid (Fig. 38).	$\dfrac{na:a:pa:mc}{2}$	12	dihexagonal pyramid
3rd order prism (Fig. 39)....	$\dfrac{na:a:pa:\infty c}{2}$	6	dihexagonal prism
1st order pyramid (Fig. 25).	$\dfrac{a:a:\infty a:mc}{2}$	12	1st order pyramid
1st order prism (Fig. 26)....	$\dfrac{a:a:\infty a:\infty c}{2}$	6	1st order prism
2nd order pyramid (Fig. 27)	$\dfrac{2a:a:2a:mc}{2}$	12	2nd order pyramid
2nd order prism (Fig. 28)...	$\dfrac{2a:a:2a:\infty c}{2}$	6	2nd order prism
Basal-pinacoid (Fig. 31).....	$\dfrac{\infty a:\infty a:\infty a:c}{2}$	2	basal-pinacoid

Synonyms for the Names of the Pyramidal Hemihedral Hexagonal Forms.

3rd order pyramid — 3rd order bipyramid.

3rd order prism — none.

Method of Determining Pyramidal Hemihedral Hexagonal Forms by the Use of Symbols.

After properly orienting the crystal in the manner already described all the forms but the 3rd order pyramid and prism may be identified easily by applying the rules already given for the determination of holohedral forms of the same name. 3rd order pyramids and prisms may be recognized by determining the symbol of any face in the manner already described in the discussion of holohedral forms, dividing this symbol by 2, and then ascertaining from the table the name of the form possessing this symbol.

Suggestions for Attaining Facility in the Recognition of Forms.

Orient the crystal and determine which of the following descriptions (which should be learned at once) apply to the face or faces of different shape or size seen. It is possible, but unnecessary, to distinguish between + and − forms in this division. It is assumed that the student is already familiar with the rules for recognizing those forms identical in shape and position with the holohedral ones (see p. 51).

3rd order pyramid: A face sloping down from the vertical axis so that its plane intersects all three horizontal crystal axes at unequal finite distances from the origin.

The 3rd order pyramid differs in no way from the 1st or 2nd order pyramid excepting in position with respect to the horizontal crystal axes. All three types of 12-faced pyramids may have the same appearance; and any such pyramid may be held at will as a 1st, 2nd, or 3rd order pyramid. The 3rd order pyramid is skewed or twisted through

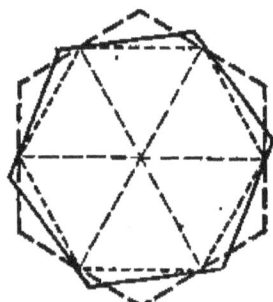

FIG. 40. — Diagram showing the relations of the 1st order (dotted lines), 2nd order (broken lines), and 3rd order (solid lines) pyramids and prisms to the horizontal crystal axes.

a small angle (less than 30°) either to the right or left away from the position of the 1st or 2nd order pyramid. Fig. 40 shows how the horizontal axes are cut by 1st, 2nd, and 3rd order pyramids and prisms.

3rd order prism: A vertical face whose plane intersects the three horizontal crystal axes at unequal finite distances from the origin.

All that was said in the preceding section relative to the 3rd order pyramid applies with equal truth to the 3rd order prism.

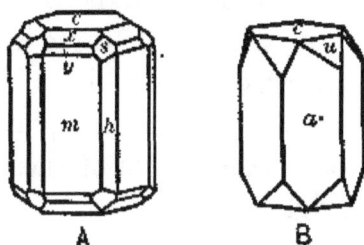

FIG. 41. — Pyramidal hemihedral hexagonal crystals.

A: Basal-pinacoid (*c*), 1st order prism (*m*), two 1st order pyramids (*x* and *y*), 2nd order pyramid (*s*), and 3rd order prism (*h*).

B: Basal-pinacoid (*c*), 2nd order prism (*a*), and 3rd order pyramid (*u*).

TRIGONAL HEMIHEDRAL DIVISION

Development or Derivation of the Forms.

Trigonal hemihedral hexagonal forms may be conceived to be developed by dividing each of the holohedral forms by means of the three secondary symmetry planes containing the horizontal crystal axes into six parts, then suppressing all faces lying wholly within alternate parts thus obtained, and extending the remaining faces until they meet in edges or corners.

Symmetry.

The trigonal hemihedral division of the hexagonal system is characterized by the presence of one principal and three interchangeable secondary symmetry planes which lie at right angles to the principal

41

symmetry plane. The interchangeable symmetry planes make angles of 60° or 120° with each other.

Selection, Position, and Designation of the Crystal Axes.

The principal symmetry axis is chosen as the vertical or *c* crystal axis; while three interchangeable horizontal directions, each of which bisects the angle between two secondary symmetry planes, constitute the horizontal or *a* axes. One of these is so held as to extend from right to left.

Orienting Crystals.

Trigonal hemihedral forms are oriented by holding the principal symmetry plane horizontally, and one secondary symmetry plane vertically and extending from front to back. The crystal axes will then extend in the proper direction.

Trigonal Hemihedral Hexagonal Forms Tabulated.

Name.	Symbol.	Number of faces.	Form from which derived.
± 1st order trigonal pyramid (Fig. 42)	$\pm \dfrac{a : a : \infty a : mc}{2}$	6	1st order pyramid
± 1st order trigonal prism (Fig. 43)	$\pm \dfrac{a : a : \infty a : \infty c}{2}$	3	1st order prism
Ditrigonal pyramid (Fig. 44)	$\dfrac{na : a : pa : mc}{2}$	12	dihexagonal pyramid
Ditrigonal prism (Fig. 45)	$\dfrac{na : a : pa : \infty c}{2}$	6	dihexagonal prism
2nd order pyramid (Fig. 27)	$\dfrac{2a : a : 2a : mc}{2}$	12	2nd order pyramid
2nd order prism (Fig. 28)	$\dfrac{2a : a : 2a : \infty c}{2}$	6	2nd order prism
Basal-pinacoid (Fig. 31)	$\dfrac{\infty a : \infty a : \infty a : c}{2}$	2	basal-pinacoid

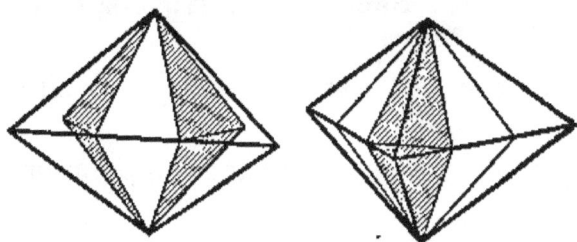

FIG. 42. — Positive (on left) and negative (on right) 1st order trigonal pyramids containing the forms from which they are derived. The suppressed faces are shaded.

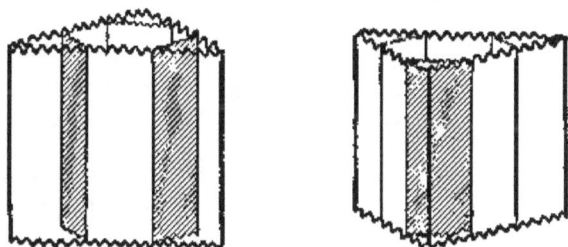

FIG. 43. — Positive (on left) and negative (on right) 1st order trigonal prisms containing the forms from which they are derived. The suppressed faces are shaded.

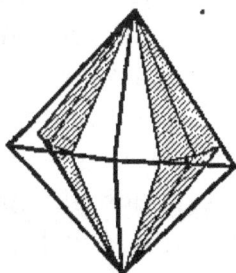

FIG. 44. — Ditrigonal pyramid containing the form from which it is derived. The suppressed faces are shaded.

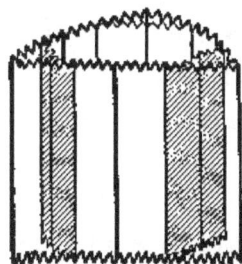

FIG. 45.— Ditrigonal prism containing the form from which it is derived. The suppressed faces are shaded.

Synonyms for the Names of the Trigonal Hemihedral Hexagonal Forms.

1st order trigonal pyramid — trigonal bipyramid of the 1st order.

Ditrigonal pyramid — ditrigonal bipyramid.

Positive and Negative Forms Distinguished.

All those forms produced by the suppression of faces lying within the same set of alternating dodecants are said to be of the same sign ($+$ or $-$). It is possible, but unnecessary, to distinguish between $+$ and $-$ ditrigonal pyramids and prisms. It is customary to consider a trigonal prism or pyramid with a face or faces extending from right to left between the vertical axis and the observer as $+$, while one with such a face or faces back of the vertical axis is $-$. In reality, a $+$ trigonal pyramid differs in no way from a $-$ trigonal pyramid excepting in position; and a trigonal pyramid may be held in either the $+$ or $-$ position at will. The same statements hold as regards the trigonal prism. Convention requires that the largest and most prominent trigonal pyramid or prism should be held in such a way as to bring it into the $+$ position.

All the other statements regarding $+$ and $-$ forms made in the discussion of the rhombohedral hemihedral division (see p. 57) apply with equal truth to the division under consideration.

Method of Determining Trigonal Hemihedral Hexagonal Forms by the Use of Symbols.

After properly orienting the crystal in the manner already described the 2nd order pyramid and prism

44

and the basal-pinacoid may be identified easily by applying the rules already given for the determination of holohedral forms of the same name.

The four hemihedral forms differing in shape from the holohedral ones from which they were derived may be recognized by determining the symbol of any face in the manner described in the discussion of holohedral forms, dividing this symbol by 2, and then ascertaining from the table the name of the form possessing this symbol.

Suggestions for Attaining Facility in the Recognition of Forms.

Orient the crystal and determine which of the following descriptions (which should be learned at once) apply to the face or faces of different shape or size seen. It is assumed that the student is already familiar with the rules for recognizing those forms identical in shape with the holohedral ones (see p. 51).

+ *1st order trigonal pyramid:* A face sloping down from the vertical axis directly toward the observer. This face occupies exactly the same position as that of a + rhombohedron. However, a 1st order trigonal pyramid differs from a rhombohedron in that the three faces at one end of the vertical axis intersect those at the other end in edges which are horizontal.

− *1st order trigonal pyramid:* A face sloping down from the vertical axis directly away from the observer at the back of the crystal. This face occupies exactly the same position as that of a − rhombohedron.

+ *1st order trigonal prism:* A vertical face extending directly from right to left between the vertical axis and the observer.

— *1st order trigonal prism:* A vertical face extending directly from right to left at the back of the crystal.

Ditrigonal pyramid: A face sloping down from the vertical axis in such a way that its plane intersects the three horizontal crystal axes at unequal finite distances from the origin. The six faces at each end of the vertical axis occupy exactly the same positions as the six faces making up half of a scalenohedron, but may be distinguished from scalenohedron faces by the fact that the faces at opposite

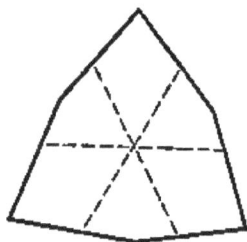

FIG. 46. — Diagram showing the relation of the faces of the trigonal hemihedral ditrigonal pyramid and prism to the horizontal crystal axes. (Compare with Fig. 54.)

ends of the vertical axis intersect in edges that are horizontal.

Ditrigonal prism: A vertical face whose plane intersects all three horizontal crystal axes at unequal finite distances from the origin.

Hemimorphism.

A hemimorphic crystal, as already stated (p. 17), is one in which the law of axes (see p. 16) is violated so far as one crystal axis is concerned. In other words, on a hemimorphic crystal the opposite ends of one crystal axis are not cut by the same number of similarly placed faces. For instance, there may be one or more pyramids on one end of a crystal axis, and only a basal pinacoid on the other; or the forms at both ends of an axis may have the same names, but different slopes.

Theoretically, hemimorphic forms may occur in all divisions of the hexagonal system, but they are relatively unimportant on any kind of crystals already discussed excepting trigonal hemihedral hexagonal ones.

Naming Hemimorphic Forms.

It is customary to hold the axis whose ends are treated differently vertically. After properly orienting the crystal the forms on the upper end of the crystal are given first, then the crystal is turned upside down, and those on the other end are named. Forms common to both ends, like prisms and pinacoids (other than the basal pinacoid), are mentioned but once.

In writing out the names of the forms on a hemimorphic crystal it is customary to separate the names of the forms on the differing ends of the crystal by means of a horizontal line.

Importance of Hemimorphism in the Trigonal Hemihedral Hexagonal Division.

With one possible exception, all natural minerals crystallizing in this division of the hexagonal system are hemimorphic, that is, the opposite ends of their vertical axes are not intersected by the same number of similar faces similarly placed. This eliminates the principal symmetry plane, and gives the trigonal and ditrigonal pyramids the appearance of rhombohedrons and scalenohedrons. That the crystals resulting are not rhombohedral is, however, usually shown plainly by the presence of a prominent trigonal prism, a form which does not occur in the rhombohedral hemihedral division. This gives trig-

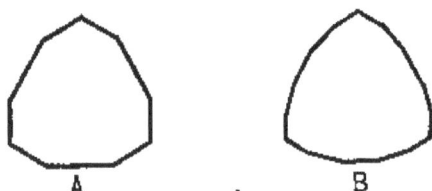

Fig. 47. — Typical horizontal sections of the trigonal hemihedral mineral tourmaline.

onal hemihedral crystals cross-sections which are either triangular or (more commonly) spherical-triangular. Fig. 47 shows two typical cross-sections of the mineral tourmaline which is the commonest species crystallizing in this division of the system.

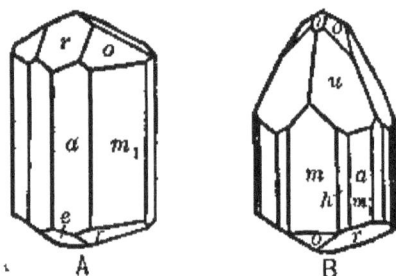

Fig. 48. — Trigonal hemihedral hexagonal crystals (hemimorphic).

A: $+$ and $-$1st order trigonal pyramids (r and o), $-$1st order trigonal prism (m_1), and 2nd order prism (a). On other end: $+$ and $-$1st order trigonal pyramids (r and e).

B: $+$ and $-$1st order trigonal pyramids (r and o), $+$ and $-$1st order trigonal prisms (m and m_1), ditrigonal pyramid (u), ditrigonal prism (h), and 2nd order prism (a). On other end: $+$ and $-$1st order trigonal pyramids (r and o).

TRAPEZOHEDRAL HEMIHEDRAL DIVISION

Trapezohedral hemihedral forms may be conceived to be developed by dividing each holohedral form by the principal and all the secondary symmetry planes into 24 parts, then suppressing all faces lying wholly within alternate parts thus obtained, and extending all the remaining faces until they meet in edges or corners.

As the dihexagonal pyramid is the only hexagonal form with 24 faces, it is evident that a dihexagonal pyramid face is the only one that can lie' wholly within one of the parts obtained by dividing a hexagonal crystal in the manner just specified. The dihexagonal pyramid is, then, the only hexagonal form from which a trapezohedral hemihedral form differing from the holohedral one in shape and name can be derived. This new form is called the hexagonal trapezohedron (Fig. 49). This form may be either right or left-handed, but, since no mineral is known to crystallize in this division, its further discussion seems unnecessary.

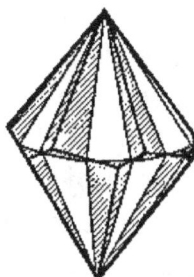

Fig. 49. — Hexagonal trapezohedron containing the form from which it is derived. The suppressed faces are shaded.

TRAPEZOHEDRAL TETARTOHEDRAL DIVISION

Development or Derivation of the Forms.

Trapezohedral tetartohedral hexagonal forms may be conceived to be developed by the simultaneous application of the rhombohedral and trapezohedral hemihedrisms. In other words, a holohedral form is first divided into dodecants by means of the principal symmetry plane and the three secondary symmetry planes containing the crystal axes, as in the development of rhombohedral hemihedral forms; and faces or portions of faces lying within alternating dodecants arc marked tentatively as subject to suppression. The holohedral form is then divided by means of the principal and all of the secondary symmetry planes into twenty-four parts, as in the development of trapezohedral hemihedral forms; and faces or portions of faces lying within alternating parts thus obtained are marked tentatively as subject to suppression. If, after this has been done, it is found that any crystal face has been marked in such a way as to indicate that all portions of it are tentatively subject to suppression, that

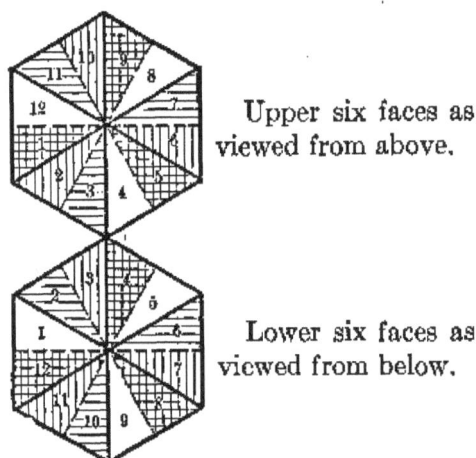

Upper six faces as viewed from above.

Lower six faces as viewed from below.

Fig. 50. — Diagram to illustrate the development of the 2nd order trigonal pyramid from the 2nd order pyramid as explained in the text.

crystal face is suppressed; but, if all or any portion of a crystal face remains unmarked as subject to suppression, that face is extended until it meets other similar faces in edges or corners.

As an illustration of the process just outlined, consider a 2nd order pyramid (see Fig. 50). If this form is divided by means of the principal symmetry

50

plane and the secondary symmetry planes containing the crystal axes, and faces or parts of faces lying within alternating dodecants thus obtained are marked tentatively as subject to suppression, parts of faces 1 and 2, 5 and 6, and 9 and 10 on top of the crystal; and 3 and 4, 7 and 8, and 11 and 12 on the other end should be so marked, as indicated by the vertically hatched portions on Fig. 50. If, then, the form be divided by means of the principal symmetry plane and all six secondary symmetry planes into twenty-four parts, and faces or parts of faces lying within alternating parts thus obtained be marked tentatively as subject to suppression, the parts of the faces so marked will be those num-

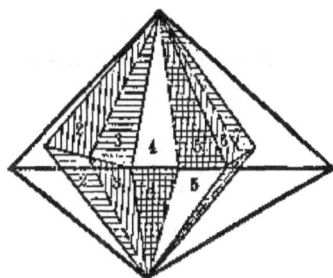

FIG. 51. — 2nd order trigonal pyramid containing the form from which it is derived. Suppressed faces are shaded.

bered 1, 3; 5, 7, 9, and 11 on top of the crystal, and 2, 4, 6, 8, 10, and 12 on the bottom, as indicated by the horizontally hatched portions in Fig. 50. This leaves the half-faces 4, 8, and 12, on top, and the half-faces 1, 5, and 9, on the other end of the crystal unhatched, while all the remaining faces are completely hatched. If, then, we extend the faces partially unhatched until they meet in edges or corners as illustrated by Fig. 51, we shall obtain the trapezohedral tetartohedral derivative of the second order pyramid, namely, the 2nd order trigonal pyramid. By applying this method to the other holohedral forms, their trapezohedral tetartohedral derivatives may be ascertained.

51

Symmetry.

Trapezohedral tetartohedral forms possess no symmetry planes whatever, but show a three-fold or six-fold arrangement of faces.

Selection, Position, and Designation of the Crystal Axes.

The four directions used as crystal axes in the holohedral division are still utilized for the same purpose in the trapezohedral tetartohedral division. In other words, one vertical or c axis and three interchangeable horizontal or a axes intersecting at angles of 60° or 120° are utilized. One of the latter is held from right to left.

Orienting Crystals.

The absence of all symmetry planes, and the presence of two sets of prominent interchangeable crystallographic directions which may be so placed as to occupy the position of the horizontal crystal axes makes it impossible to give any rules for orienting trapezohedral tetartohedral crystals based entirely on symmetry planes or crystallographic directions.

Since quartz is the only mineral which occurs at all commonly in recognizable trapezohedral tetartohedral crystals, it seems best to suggest rules for orientation applicable especially to that mineral. These are as follows:

On most crystals one crystallographic direction emerging on the surface of the crystal at a corner formed by the intersection of three or six faces making equal angles with each other is usually very prominent. This is selected as the vertical or c axis, and is not interchangeable with any other crystallographic direction. The crystal is then rotated around the vertical axis until prominent prism faces occupy the 1st order position; or, if a prominent prism is lacking, prominent pyramidal faces are placed in the 1st order position. The three interchangeable horizontal crystal axes will then extend in the proper directions.

Trapezohedral Tetartohedral Hexagonal Forms Tabulated.

Name.	Symbol.	Number of faces.	Form from which derived.
± Rhombohedron (Fig. 34).	$\pm \dfrac{a:a:\infty a:mc}{4}$	6	1st order pyramid
±2nd order trigonal pyramid (Fig. 51)	$\pm \dfrac{2a:a:2a:mc}{4}$	6	2nd order pyramid
±2nd order trigonal prism (Fig. 52)	$\pm \dfrac{2a:a:2a:\infty c}{4}$	3	2nd order prism
Trigonal trapezohedron (Fig. 53)	$\dfrac{na:a:pa:mc}{4}$	6	dihexagonal pyramid
Ditrigonal prism (Fig. 54)	$\dfrac{na:a:pa:\infty c}{4}$	6	dihexagonal prism
1st order prism (Fig. 26)	$\dfrac{a:a:\infty a:\infty c}{4}$	6	1st order prism
Basal-pinacoid (Fig. 31)	$\dfrac{\infty a:\infty a:\infty a:c}{4}$	2	basal-pinacoid

Synonyms for the Names of the Trapezohedral Tetartohedral Hexagonal Forms.

2nd order trigonal pyramid — trigonal bipyramid of the 2nd order.

2nd order trigonal prism — unsymmetrical trigonal prism.

Trigonal trapezohedron — quadrilateral trapezohedron.

Positive and Negative Forms Distinguished.

It is possible to distinguish between + and − variations of each of the trapezohedral tetartohedral forms which differ in shape from the holohedral ones

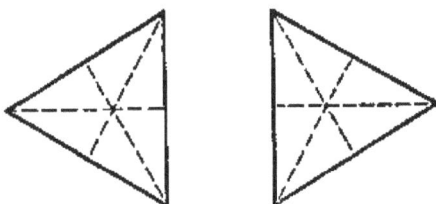

FIG. 52. — Diagrams showing relations of the positive (on left) and negative (on right) 2nd order trigonal pyramid and prism to the horizontal crystal axes.

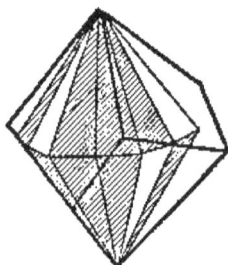

FIG. 53. — Trigonal trapezohedron containing the form from which it is derived. The suppressed faces are shaded.

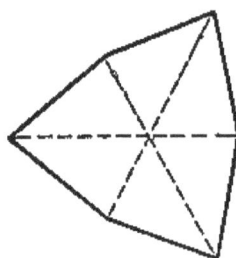

FIG. 54. — Diagram showing the relation of the tetartohedral ditrigonal prism to the horizontal crystal axes.

from which they are derived. It is, however, unnecessary to differentiate between + and − trigonal trapezohedrons and ditrigonal prisms.

+ and − rhombohedrons are distinguished in exactly the same way as are + and − rhombohedrons in the rhombohedral hemihedral division (see p. 56).

It is customary to call those trigonal prisms and pyramids + which have a face or faces extending directly from front to back at the *right* of the vertical axes; while those with a similar face or faces at the *left* of the vertical axis are called −. See Fig. 52.

Symbols of Tetartohedral Forms.

The symbol of a tetartohedral form in any system is the same as that of the holohedral form from which it is derived excepting that it is written as a fraction with the figure 4 as the denominator. This does not mean that, in the case of the tetartohedral forms, the axes are intersected at one-fourth the holohedral axial lengths, but is merely a conventional method of indicating that the symbol is that of a quarter (tetartohedral) form. The symbol $\dfrac{na : a : pa : mc}{4}$ is read *na, a, pa, mc* over 4.

Method of Determining Trapezohedral Tetartohedral Hexagonal Forms by the Use of Symbols.

After properly orienting the crystal the 1st order prism and basal-pinacoid may be identified easily by applying the rules already given for the determination of holohedral forms of the same name. The tetartohedral forms new in shape may be recognized by determining the symbol of any face in the manner described in the discussion of holohedral forms, dividing this symbol by 4, and then ascertaining from the table the name of the form possessing this symbol.

Suggestions for Attaining Facility in the Recognition of Forms.

Orient the crystal and determine which of the following descriptions (which should be learned at once) apply to the face or faces of different shape or size seen. It is assumed that the student is already familiar with the rules for recognizing those forms identical in shape with the holohedral ones (see p. 51).

± *Rhombohedron:* Since the trapezohedral tetartohedral rhombohedrons differ in no way excepting in internal molecular arrangement from the rhombohedral hemihedral forms of the same name, rules for the recognition of the + and − rhombohedrons given in the description of rhombohedral hemihedral forms (see p. 57) may be used in identifying such forms in this division.

+ *2nd order trigonal pyramid:* A face which slopes down from the vertical axis directly to the right.

The 2nd order trigonal pyramid does not differ in appearance from the 1st order trigonal pyramid occurring in the trigonal hemihedral division, but does differ from the latter in its position with reference to the horizontal crystal axes.

− *2nd order trigonal pyramid:* A face which slopes down from the vertical axis directly to the left.

+ *2nd order trigonal prism:* A vertical face extending from front to back at the right of the vertical axis.

· The 2nd order trigonal prism does not differ in appearance from the 1st order trigonal prism occurring in the trigonal hemihedral division, but does differ from the latter in its position with reference to the horizontal crystal axes.

— *2nd order trigonal prism:* A vertical face extending from front to back at the left of the vertical axis.

Trigonal trapezohedron: A face sloping down from the vertical axis in such a way that its plane intersects all three horizontal crystal axes at unequal finite distances from the origin.

It is possible, but not necessary, to distinguish between right- and left-handed trigonal trapezohedrons.

The trigonal trapezohedron, like the 1st and 2nd order trigonal pyramids and the rhombohedron, has three faces at each end of the vertical axis, but the faces on top do not intersect those below in horizontal edges, as is the case with the trigonal pyramid; nor is a face on top directly above an edge below, as is the case with the rhombohedron. The three faces on one end appear, in fact, to have been twisted around the vertical axis through a small angle (less than 30°) to the right or left, placing them in an unsymmetrical position with reference to those at the other end of the crystal.

The trigonal trapezohedron is most apt to be confused with a 2nd order trigonal pyramid. These may usually be distinguished easily if the following tests are applied:

If a vertical plane is passed through an edge between two equally steep 1st order faces, it will bisect the angle between two diverging edges of a 2nd order trigonal pyramid face directly above or below the edge first mentioned. Equally steep 1st order faces in this division of the system are those of the 1st order prism, and, in the case of quartz, those between the most prominent + and − rhombohedrons.

The statement just made will not be found true where trigonal trapezohedrons lie over or under the edges formed by the intersection of equally steep 1st order faces.

Ditrigonal prism: The tetartohedral ditrigonal prism closely resembles the trigonal hemihedral form of the same name (see p. 66), but differs therefrom in that it appears to have a symmetry plane running from right to left (see Fig. 54), while the hemihedral form has a symmetry plane extending from front to back (see Fig. 46).

General Observations.

It has already been mentioned that quartz is the only common mineral crystallizing in this division, of the hexagonal system, and it should be noted that the crystallization of quartz is peculiar in that the most prominent faces are a 1st order prism (sometimes missing) and an equally or unequally developed + and − rhombohedron the faces of which make equal angles with the prism faces. In the absence of other forms, the combination last mentioned appears to be rhombohedral hemihedral, while the first combination appears to be holohedral. The presence of either a trigonal trapezohedron or trigonal pyramid is sufficient to prove the crystal tetartohedral, but these forms are very rare. The trigonal and ditrigonal prisms and basal-pinacoid are almost never found on quartz crystals.

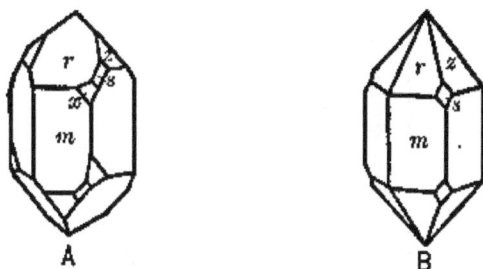

Fig. 55. — Trapezohedral tetartohedral hexagonal crystals.

A: + and − rhombohedrons (*r* and *z*), 1st order prism (*m*), − 2nd order trigonal pyramid (*s*), and trigonal trapezohedron (*x*).

B: + and − rhombohedron (*r* and *z*) equally developed, 1st order prism (*m*), and − 2nd order trigonal pyramid (*s*).

Application of the Law Governing Combination of Forms.

It has already been mentioned that one of the commonest mistakes made in determining crystal forms is the naming of two or more forms which cannot possibly occur on the same crystal since their presence would be in direct violation of the law governing the combination of forms (see p. 36). The student should thoroughly familiarize himself with the table on p. 83 if he wishes to avoid the mistake mentioned.

Inspection of this table will show that the basal-pinacoid is the only form that occurs unchanged in all five of the divisions tabulated. It is, then, the only form that can be combined with any other of the forms in the divisions considered. Further, it should be noticed that the 1st order prism occurs unchanged in all divisions but the trigonal hemihedral, while the 2nd order pyramid and prism occur unchanged in all divisions but the trapezohedral tetartohedral. The forms in the 3rd

59

Holohedral forms.	Rhombohedral hemihedral forms.	Pyramidal hemihedral forms.	Trigonal hemihedral forms.	Trapezohedral tetartohedral forms.
1st order pyramid......	rhombohedron	1st order pyramid	1st order trigonal pyramid	rhombohedron
1st order prism.........	1st order prism	1st order prism	1st order trigonal prism	1st order prism
2nd order pyramid.....	2nd order pyramid	2nd order pyramid	2nd order pyramid	2nd order trigonal pyramid
2nd order prism........	2nd order prism	2nd order prism	2nd order prism	2nd order trigonal prism
Dihexagonal pyramid ..	hexagonal scalenohedron	3rd order pyramid	ditrigonal pyramid	trigonal trapezohedron
Dihexagonal prism	dihexagonal prism	3rd order prism	ditrigonal prism	ditrigonal prism
Basal-pinacoid	basal-pinacoid	basal-pinacoid	basal-pinacoid	basal-pinacoid

60

order position are apt to give the most trouble, since the dihexagonal pyramid yields a form of new name and shape in each of the hemihedral and tetartohedral divisions; while the dihexagonal prism yields a form of new name and shape in all divisions but the rhombohedral hemihedral.

RHOMBOHEDRAL TETARTOHEDRAL DIVISION

Rhombohedral tetartohedral forms may be conceived to be developed by the simultaneous application of the rhombohedral and pyramidal hemihedrisms, according to the principles outlined in the discussion of the trapezohedral tetartohedral hexagonal division (see p. 72). The names of the resulting rhombohedral tetartohedral forms together with their symbols, number of faces, and the name of the corresponding holohedral forms are shown on the following table:

Name.	Symbol.	Number of faces.	Form from which derived.
1st order rhombohedron..	$\dfrac{a:a:\infty a:mc}{4}$	6	1st order pyramid
2nd order rhombohedron.	$\dfrac{2a:a:2a:mc}{4}$	6	2nd order pyramid
3rd order rhombohedron..	$\dfrac{na:a:pa:mc}{4}$	6	dihexagonal pyramid
3rd order prism..........	$\dfrac{na:a:pa:\infty c}{4}$	6	dihexagonal prism
1st order prism..........	$\dfrac{a:a:\infty a:\infty c}{4}$	6	1st order prism
2nd order prism..........	$\dfrac{2a:a:2a:\infty c}{4}$	6	2nd order prism
Basal-pinacoid..........	$\dfrac{\infty a:\infty a:\infty a:c}{4}$	2	basal-pinacoid

The rhombohedral tetartohedral 3rd order prism is exactly like the form of the same name in the pyramidal hemihedral division (see p. 63). The 1st order rhombohedron is exactly like the rhombohedron occurring in the rhombohedral hemihedral and the trapezohedral tetartohedral divisions; while the 2nd and 3rd order rhombohedrons differ from the 1st order form of the same name only in position with reference to the crystal axes. The former is, of course, in the 2nd order position, while the latter is in the 3rd order position.

Further consideration of this division seems unnecessary since few minerals are rhombohedral tetartohedral, and these are comparatively rare.

Table of Hexagonal Symbols Used by Various Authorities.

	Weiss.	Naumann.	Dana.	Miller.
1st order pyramid.........	$a : a : \infty a : mc$	mP	m	$(h0\bar{h}i)$
1st order prism.............	$a : a : \infty a : \infty c$	∞P	I	$(10\bar{1}0)$
2nd order pyramid........	$2a : a : 2a : mc$	$mP2$	$m-2$	$(hh2h2i)$
2nd order prism...........	$2a : a : 2a : \infty c$	$\infty P2$	$i-2$	$(10\bar{2}0)$
Dihexagonal pyramid......	$na : a : pa : mc$	mPn	$m-n$	$(hk\bar{l}i)$
Dihexagonal prism........	$na : a : pa : \infty c$	∞Pn	$i-n$	$(hk\bar{l}0)$
Basal-pinacoid.............	$\infty a : \infty a : \infty a : c$	$0P$	O	(0001)

Weiss, Naumann, and Dana divide the holohedral symbols by 2 and by 4 when referring to hemihedral and tetartohedral forms, respectively. Miller prefixes various Greek letters when forming the symbols of hemihedral and tetartohedral forms.

www.ingramcontent.com/pod-product-compliance
Lightning Source LLC
Chambersburg PA
CBHW020358270326
41926CB00007B/500